Published by Concordia Publishing House
3558 S. Jefferson Avenue, St. Louis, MO 63118-3968
1-800-325-3040 • www.cph.org

Text © 2009 Marilyn Sommerer
Illustrations © 2009 by Concordia Publishing House

Manufactured in China

1 2 3 4 5 6 7 8 9 10   18 17 16 15 14 13 12 11 10 09

The First Christmas Present

Story by Marilyn Sommerer

Art by Johanna van der Sterre

CONCORDIA PUBLISHING HOUSE · SAINT LOUIS

The first Christmas present
was given by a father.

A mother wrapped the first Christmas present, but she did not wrap it with paper and ribbon.

The father put someone in charge of the present to keep it safe.

On the night when the father gave
the first Christmas present, the first
Christmas carol was sung.

Do you know what the first
Christmas present was?

Yes! The little baby
Jesus was the very first
Christmas present.

God was the Father who gave Jesus to all of us to be our best Friend and our Savior.

Mary was the mother who wrapped the first Christmas present in swaddling clothes. She wanted Him to feel safe and snug and warm.

Joseph was the man God chose to take care of the new baby and His mother.

The first Christmas carol was a song that was sung by a choir of angels. The only people who heard their song were poor shepherds who were out in the fields watching over their sheep.

The angels sang, "Glory to God in the highest, and on earth peace . . ." The angels were singing about how great God is because He loved us enough to send Jesus.

Did you ever give a present to a Present? Some Wise Men did! They saw a big, sparkly star in the night sky, and they followed it. They traveled a long, long way so they could give presents to Jesus.

You can bring presents to Jesus too.
He isn't a baby anymore. There's
nothing you can buy in a store and
send up to Him in heaven.

So, what do you think He would like you
to give Him?

Well, Jesus loves to hear His children sing to Him. Will you give Him a song?

Jesus loves to hear His children talk to Him. Will you give Him a prayer?

Jesus loves to see His children loving one another. Will you do something kind and good for someone?

If you do these things, you are giving Jesus the Christmas present He wants the most . . . your heart filled with faith and love.

Now we can have peace
in our hearts because
we know Jesus loves us,
saves us, and will take us
to heaven someday. What
a wonderful Christmas
present! It will last forever
and ever.